Hat Cha

Hats and Caps

There are many different kinds of hats and caps, but they all go on heads.

3

Hard Hats and Helmets

Hard hats and helmets can protect people when they are working or playing.

4

Firefighter's helmet

Hats That Work

Many people wear uniforms at work. A uniform often includes a hat.

6

Special Hats

Sometimes people wear hats
when they dress up.
They might wear a hat
for a special event,
or just for fun!

8

Mexican festival hats

9

Historical Hats

People have worn hats all through history.

Chinese hat
(1800s)

 # Hats Around the World

Hats from around the world come in many styles.

13

Make Your Own Hat!

paint and
a brush

large piece
of paper

tape

scissors

1 Cut a half circle
from the piece of paper.

14

2 Bend the shape
to make a cone.
Tape the edges
in place.

3 Decorate
your hat!

Index